Contents

Who was Mary Cassatt?

Mary Cassatt was an American artist. She was a successful woman painter at a time when most painters were men.

Most of Mary's art shows **scenes** from everyday life. Some of her most well-known paintings are of mothers and children.

Early years

Mary was born on 22 May 1844 in Pittsburgh, America. When Mary was seven years old she moved to Paris in France with her family. Two years later they moved to Germany. She was ten years old when this picture was drawn.

At school, Mary **studied** many subjects. She liked drawing and music. She drew whatever was around her. She liked to draw pictures of her family. Mary painted this **portrait** of her mother, Katherine Cassatt, in 1889.

Art student in Philadelphia

In 1855, Mary and her family moved back to America. When Mary was 17 years old she went to the Pennsylvania Academy of Fine Arts. Mary is the girl on the right.

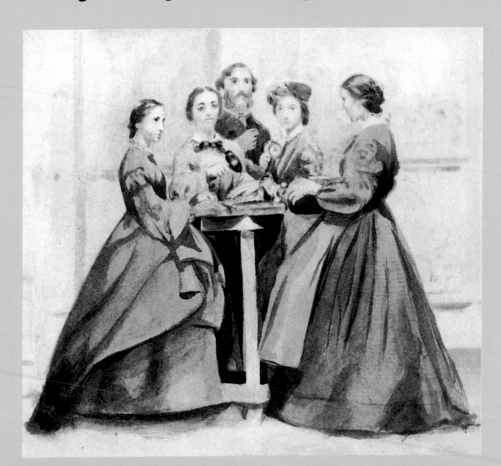

Mary learned to draw from life and by **studying** other works of art. She liked to ride horses with her older brother, Alexander. This is a **portrait** Mary painted of him when she was 36 years old.

Paris

In 1866 Mary went to Paris. She wanted to **study** art. Like other art students, she studied works of art by great artists. She copied their paintings in a museum called the Louvre.

Mary studied **Madonna and Child** paintings.
This helped her to paint her own pictures of
mothers caring for their small children.

The Salon

In 1868, when Mary was 24 years old, her work was chosen to be shown in the **Salon** in Paris. The Salon was a place where artists who made excellent paintings showed their work.

This painting is called 'On the Balcony during Carnival'. It is like many of the paintings Mary made when she first moved to Paris. It is the kind of painting the Salon judges liked.

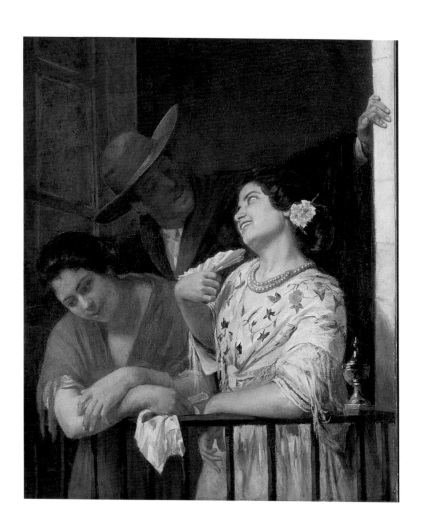

Professional artist

Mary **exhibited** in the **Salon** for a few more years. She grew tired of having to paint what would please the judges at the Salon.

Mary did not want to paint **models** anymore.
She did not want to use dark colours. She
wanted to paint things as she saw them.

Changing her ways

In 1877, Mary met an artist called Edgar Degas. Edgar introduced Mary to other painters. These painters were known as the **Impressionists.** The Impressionists painted **scenes** of everyday life.

The Impressionists painted with **splotches** of colour. Mary liked the colours they used and the way they used them. She made this painting in 1878 soon after she met Edgar.

Joining the Impressionists

Mary and Edgar became good friends. They visited each other's **studios**. They talked about their work and gave each other ideas. Edgar Degas painted this **portrait** of Mary.

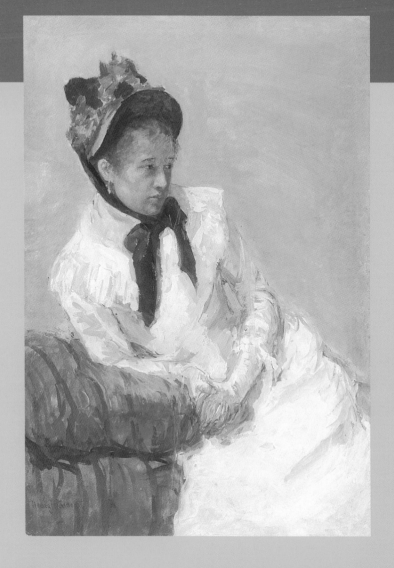

Mary liked the **Impressionists'** ideas. She used their ideas in her own paintings. She began to use lighter colours and looser brushstrokes. She did this **self-portrait** in 1878.

Painting real life

Most **Impressionists** painted outdoor **scenes**. Mary used the Impressionist ideas but she painted indoor scenes. The paintings tell us about Mary's life.

Most of Mary's paintings are **portraits** of her family, friends and neighbours. Many things in Mary's paintings belonged to her. Look at the silver tea set on page 20. You can see it in the painting on this page.

Painting women

Mary lived in a lively part of Paris near this café. Painters, musicians, and writers met at cafés to talk about their ideas. Mary and the women she knew read newspapers. They wanted to keep up with the news.

Mary sometimes painted women reading the newspaper. This was something new in painting. At that time, most artists painted **models** who **posed** just for the painting.

Mothers and children

Mary never married or had any children. Mary's brother, Alexander, and his family stayed with her when they visited Europe. Mary loved her nieces and nephews. She often painted pictures of them.

Mary spent hours on each drawing and painting. Yet much of her work shows **scenes** that would be over very quickly. This is a painting of a mother washing her sleepy child.

French countryside

Mary bought a house near Paris. She spent most of her time there. Her **studio** was on the first floor of her home. She could look out onto her pond and gardens.

This picture of ducks was **inspired** by the pond behind Mary's home. This picture is a print. A print allows an artist to make many copies of the same picture. Mary worked hard and became very good at making prints.

A lasting impression

During the last years of Mary's life, her eyesight failed. She could not paint. Mary Cassatt died on 14 June 1926. She was 82 years old.

Mary Cassatt is remembered for her tender pictures of mothers and children.

Timeline

1844   Mary Cassatt born on 22 May in America.

1853   The artist Vincent van Gogh is born in Holland.

1861   Mary begins her studies at Pennsylvania
            Academy of Fine Arts.

1861–65 U. S. Civil War.

1865–70 Mary travels in Europe.

1868   Mary's work first **exhibited** at the Salon.

1879   Mary exhibits with the **Impressionists**.
            The artist Paul Klee is born.

1890   The artist Vincent van Gogh dies.

1893   Mary's first individual exhibition.

1900   World's Fair in Paris, France.

1914–18 The First World War.
            Mary moves to Italy to avoid the war.

1920   Women in the U.S. win the right to vote.

1926   Mary Cassatt dies on 14 June.

Glossary

exhibit to show art in public

Impressionists group of artists who painted outside to make colourful pictures

inspire to influence or guide

Madonna and Child work of art that shows Mary and baby Jesus

model person an artist paints or draws

portrait painting, drawing, or photograph of a person

pose to sit or stand still for an artist

Salon place in Paris where artists were invited to show their artwork

scene place where something happens

self-portrait picture of the artist

splotch large spot

studio place where an artist works

study to learn

More books to read
First Impressions: Mary Cassatt,
Susan E Meyer, Harry N Abrams

What makes a Cassatt a Cassatt?,
Richard Muhlberger, Cherrytree Books

Looking at Paintings: Children, Peggy Roalf, Belitha Press

More paintings to see
The sisters, Mary Cassatt, Glasgow Art Gallery, Glasgow

Young woman sewing in the garden, Mary Cassatt, Musee d'Orsay, Paris

Mother and child against a green background, Mary Cassatt, Musee d'Orsay, Paris

Index

Roald Dahl

Dirty Beasts

illustrated by Quentin Blake

PUFFIN BOOKS

To Alfhild, Else and Asta

Find out more about Roald Dahl
by visiting the website at
roalddahl.com

PUFFIN BOOKS

Published by the Penguin Group: London, New York, Australia, Canada, India, Ireland, New Zealand and South Africa
Penguin Books Ltd, Registered Offices: 80 Strand, London WC2R 0RL, England

puffinbooks.com

Text first published in the United States of America by Farrar, Straus & Giroux 1983
This edition first published in Great Britain by Jonathan Cape Ltd 1984
Published in Puffin Books 1986, reissued 2001
This edition published 2009
004 – 10 9 8 7 6 5 4

Made and printed in China by South China Printing Company

British Library Cataloguing in Publication Data
A CIP catalogue record for this book is available from the British Library

ISBN: 978-0-141-50174-1

The Pig

In England once there lived a big
And wonderfully clever pig.
To everybody it was plain
That Piggy had a massive brain.
He worked out sums inside his head,
There was no book he hadn't read,
He knew what made an airplane fly,
He knew how engines worked and why.
He knew all this, but in the end
One question drove him round the bend:
He simply couldn't puzzle out
What LIFE was really all about.
What was the reason for his birth?
Why was he placed upon this earth?
His giant brain went round and round.
Alas, no answer could be found,
Till suddenly one wondrous night,
All in a flash, he saw the light.
He jumped up like a ballet dancer
And yelled, "By gum, I've got the answer!"

"They want my bacon slice by slice
"To sell at a tremendous price!
"They want my tender juicy chops
"To put in all the butchers' shops!
"They want my pork to make a roast
"And that's the part'll cost the most!
"They want my sausages in strings!
"They even want my chitterlings!
"The butcher's shop! The carving knife!
"That is the reason for my life!"
Such thoughts as these are not designed
To give a pig great peace of mind.

Next morning, in comes Farmer Bland,
A pail of pigswill in his hand,
And Piggy with a mighty roar,
Bashes the farmer to the floor . . .
Now comes the rather grizzly bit
So let's not make too much of it,
Except that you *must* understand
That Piggy *did eat* Farmer Bland,
He ate him up from head to toe,
Chewing the pieces nice and slow.
It took an hour to reach the feet,
Because there was so much to eat,
And when he'd finished, Pig, of course,
Felt absolutely no remorse.
Slowly he scratched his brainy head
And with a little smile, he said,
"I had a fairly powerful hunch
"That he might have me for his lunch.
"And so, because I feared the worst,
"I thought I'd better eat *him* first."

The Crocodile

No animal is half so vile
As Crocky-Wock the crocodile.
On Saturdays he likes to crunch
Six juicy children for his lunch,
And he especially enjoys
Just three of each, three girls, three boys.
He smears the boys (to make them hot)
With mustard from the mustard pot.

But mustard doesn't go with girls,
It tastes all wrong with plaits and curls.
With them, what goes extremely well
Is butterscotch and caramel.
It's such a super marvellous treat
When boys are hot and girls are sweet.
At least that's Crocky's point of view.
He ought to know. He's had a few.

That's all for now. It's time for bed
Lie down and rest your sleepy head . . .
Ssh! *Listen!* What is that I hear
Gallumphing softly up the stair?
Go lock the door and fetch my gun!
Go on, child, hurry! Quickly, run!
No, stop! Stand back! He's coming in!
Oh, look, that greasy greenish skin!
The shining teeth, the greedy smile!
It's CROCKY-WOCK, THE CROCODILE!

The Lion

The lion just adores to eat
A lot of red and tender meat,
And if you ask the lion what
Is much the tenderest of the lot,
He will not say a roast of lamb
Or curried beef or devilled ham
Or crispy pork or corned beef hash
Or sausages or mutton mash.
Then could it be a big plump hen?
He answers no. What is it, then?
Oh, lion dear, could I not make
You happy with a lovely steak?
Could I entice you from your lair
With rabbit-pie or roasted hare?
The lion smiled and shook his head.
He came up very close and said,
"The meat I am about to chew
Is neither steak nor chops. IT'S YOU."

The Scorpion

You ought to thank your lucky star
  That here in England where you are
You'll never find (or so it's said)
A scorpion inside your bed.
The scorpion's name is Stingaling,
A most repulsive ugly thing,
And I would never recommend
That you should treat him as a friend.
His scaly skin is black as black
With armour-plate upon his back.
Observe his scowling murderous face,
His wicked eyes, his lack of grace,
Note well his long and crinkly tail.
And when it starts to swish and flail,
Oh gosh! Watch out! Jump back, I say,
And run till you're a mile away.
The moment that his tail goes *swish*
He has but one determined wish,
He wants to make a sudden jump
And sting you hard upon your rump.

"What *is* the matter, darling child?
"Why do you look so tense and wild?"
"Oh mummy, underneath the sheet
"There's something moving on my feet,
"Some horrid creepy crawly thing,
"D'you think it could be Stingaling?"
"What nonsense child! You're teasing me."
"I'm not, I'm not! It's reached my knee!
"It's going . . . going up my thigh!
"Oh mummy, catch it quickly! Try!
"It's on . . . it's on my bottom now!
"It's . . . *Ow! Ow-ow! Ow-ow! OW-OW!*"

The Ant-Eater

Some wealthy folks from U.S.A.,
  Who lived near San Francisco Bay,
Possessed an only child called Roy,
A plump and unattractive boy –
Half-baked, half-witted and half-boiled,
But worst of all, most dreadfully spoiled.
Whatever Roy desired each day,
His father bought him right away –
Toy motor-cars, electric trains,
The latest model aeroplanes,
A colour television-set,
A saxophone, a clarinet,
Expensive teddy-bears that talked,
And animals that walked and squawked.
That house contained sufficient toys
To thrill a half a million boys.
(As well as this, young Roy would choose,
Two pairs a week of brand-new shoes.)
And now he stood there shouting, "What
"On earth is there I haven't got?
"How hard to think of something new!
"The choices are extremely few!"

Then added, as he scratched his ear,
"Hold it! I've got a good idea!
"I think the next thing I must get
"Should be a most peculiar pet –
"The kind that no one else has got –
"A giant ANT-EATER! Why not?"
As soon as father heard the news,
He quickly wrote to all the zoos.
"Dear Sirs," he said, "My dear keepers,
"Do any of you have ant-eaters?"
They answered by return of mail.
"Our ant-eaters are not for sale."
Undaunted, Roy's fond parent hurled
More messages across the world.
He said, "I'll pay you through the nose
"If you can get me one of those."
At last he found an Indian gent
(He lived near Delhi, in a tent),
Who said that he would sacrifice
His pet for an enormous price
(The price demanded, if you please,
Was fifty thousand gold rupees).
The ant-eater arrived half-dead.
It looked at Roy and softly said,
"I'm famished. Do you think you could
"Please give me just a little food?
"A crust of bread, a bit of meat?
"I haven't had a thing to eat
"In all the time I was at sea,
"For nobody looked after me."
Roy shouted, "No! No bread or meat!
"Go find some ants! They're what you eat!"
The starving creature crawled away.
It searched the garden night and day,
It hunted every inch of ground,
But not one single ant it found.

"I personally am not about
"To try to pull *those* prickles out.
"I think a job like this requires
"The services of Mr Myers."
I shouted, "Not the dentist! No!
"Oh mum, why don't *you* have a go?"
I begged her twice, I begged her thrice,
But grown-ups never take advice.
She said, "A dentist's very strong.
"He pulls things out the whole day long."
She drove me quickly into town,
And then they turned me upside down
Upon the awful dentist's chair,
While two strong nurses held me there.

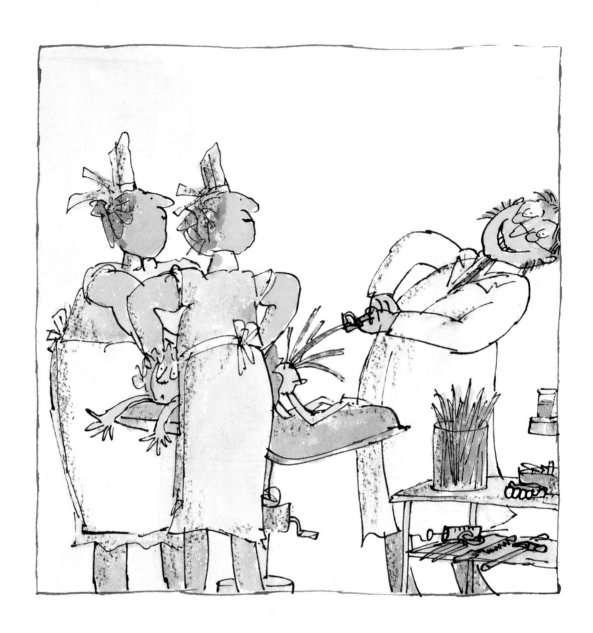

Enter the dreaded Mr Myers
Waving a massive pair of pliers.
"This is," he cried with obvious glee,
"A new experience for me.
"Quite honestly I can't pretend
"I've ever pulled things from *this* end."
He started pulling one by one
And yelling "My, oh my, what fun!"

I shouted "Help!" I shouted "Ow!"
He said, "It's nearly over now.
"For heaven's sake, don't squirm about!
"Here goes! The last one's coming out!"
The dentist pulled and out it came,
And then I heard the man exclaim,
"Let us now talk about the fees.
"That will be fifty guineas, please."
My mother is a gutsy bird
And never one to mince a word.
She cried, "By gosh, that's jolly steep!"
He answered, "No, it's very cheap.
"My dear woman, can't you see
"That if it hadn't been for me
"This child could go another year
"With prickles sticking in her rear."
So that was that. Oh, what a day!
And what a fuss! But by the way,
I think I know why porcupines
Surround themselves with prickly spines.
It is to stop some silly clown
From squashing them by sitting down.
Don't copy me. Don't be a twit.
Be sure you LOOK before you SIT.

The Cow

Please listen while I tell you now
  About a most fantastic cow.
Miss Milky Daisy was her name,
And when, aged seven months, she came
To live with us, she did her best
To look the same as all the rest.
But Daisy, as we all could see
Had some kind of deformity,
A funny sort of bumpy lump
On either side, above the rump.
Now, not so very long ago,
These bumpy lumps began to grow,
And three or maybe four months later,
(I stood there, an enthralled spectator)
These bumpy lumps burst wide apart
And out there came (I cross my heart)
Of all the wondrous marvellous things,
A pair of gold and silver wings!
A cow with wings! A flying cow!
I'd never seen one up to now.
"Oh Daisy dear, can this be true?"
She flapped her wings and up she flew!
Most gracefully she climbed up high,
She fairly whizzed across the sky.
You should have seen her dive and swoop!
She even did a loop the loop!
Of course, almost immediately
Her picture was on live T.V.,
And millions came each day to stare
At Milky Daisy in the air.
The shouted "Jeepers Creepers! Wow!
"It really is a flying cow!"
They laughed and clapped and cheered and waved,
And all of them were well-behaved

Except for one quite horrid man
Who'd travelled from Afghanistan.
This fellow, standing in the crowd,
Raised up his voice and yelled aloud,
"That silly cow! Hey, listen Daisy!"
"I think you're absolutely crazy!"
Unfortunately Daisy heard
Quite clearly every single word.
"By gosh," she cried, "what awful cheek!"
"Who is this silly foreign freak?"
She dived, and using all her power
She got to sixty miles an hour.
"Bombs gone!" she cried. "Take that!" she said,
And dropped a cowpat on his head.

The Toad and the Snail

I really am most awfully fond
  Of playing in the lily-pond.
I take off shoes and socks and coat
And paddle with my little boat.
Now yesterday, quite suddenly,
A giant toad came up to me.
This toad was easily as big
As any fair-sized fattish pig.
He smiled and said "How do you do?
"Hello! Good morning! How are you?"

(His face somehow reminded me
Of mummy's sister Emily.)
The toad said, "Don't you think I'm fine?
"Admire these lovely legs of mine,
"And I am sure you've never seen
"A toad so gloriously green!"
I said, "So far as I can see,
"You look just like Aunt Emily."
He said, "I'll bet Aunt Emily
"Can't jump one half as high as me.
"Hop on my back, young friend," he cried,
"I'll take you for a marvellous ride."
As I got on, I thought, oh blimey,
Oh, deary me. How wet and slimy!
"Sit further back," he said. "That's right.
"I'm going to jump, so hold on tight."
He jumped! Oh, how he jumped! By gum,
I thought my final hour had come!
My wretched eardrums popped and fizzed.
My eyeballs watered. Up we whizzed.
I clung on tight. I shouted, "How
"Much further are we going now?"
Toad said, his face all wreathed in smiles,
"With every jump, it's fifty miles!"
Quite literally, we jumped all over,

From Scotland to The Cliffs of Dover!
Above the Cliffs, we stopped for tea,
And Toad said, gazing at the sea,
"What do you say we take a chance,
"And jump from England into France?"
I said, "Oh dear, d'you think we oughta?
"I'd hate to finish in the water."
But toads, you'll find, don't give a wink
For what we little children think.
He didn't bother to reply.
He jumped! You should have seen us fly!
We simply soared across the sea,
The marvellous Mister Toad and me.

Then down we came, and down and down,
And landed in a funny town.
We landed hard, in fact we bounced.
"We're there! It's France!" the Toad announced.
He said, "You must admit it's grand
"To jump into a foreign land.
"No boats, no bicycles, no trains,
"No cars, no noisy aeroplanes."
Just then, we heard a fearful shout,
"Oh, heavens above!" the Toad cried out.
I turned and saw a frightening sight –
On every side, to left, to right,
People were running down the road,
Running at me and Mister Toad,
And every person, man and wife
Was brandishing a carving-knife.
It didn't take me very long
To figure there was something wrong.
And yet, how could a small boy know,
For nobody had told me so,
That Frenchmen aren't like you or me,
They do things very differently.
They won't say "yards", they call them "metres",

And they're the *most peculiar* eaters:
A Frenchman frequently regales
Himself with half-a-dozen SNAILS!
The greedy ones will gulp a score
Of these foul brutes and ask for more.
(In many of the best hotels
The people also eat the shells.)
Imagine that! My stomach turns!
One might as well eat slugs or worms!
But wait. Read on a little bit.
You haven't heard the half of it.
These French go even more agog
If someone offers them a FROG!
(You'd better fetch a basin quick
In case you're going to be sick.)
The bits of frog they like to eat
Are thighs and calves and toes and feet.
The French will gobble loads and loads
Of legs they chop off frogs and toads.
They think it's absolutely ripping
To guzzle frogs-legs fried in dripping.
That's why the whole town and their wives
Were rushing us with carving-knives.
They screamed in French, "Well I'll be blowed!
"What legs there are upon that toad!
"Chop them! Skin them! Cook them! Fry them!
"All of us are going to try them!"
"Toad!" I cried. "I'm not a funk,
"But ought we not to do a bunk?
"These rascals haven't come to greet you.
"All they want to do is eat you!"

Toad turned his head and looked at me,
And said, as cool as cool could be,
"Calm down and listen carefully please,
"I often come to France to tease
"These crazy French who long to eat
"My lovely tender froggy meat.
"I am a MAGIC TOAD!" he cried.
"And I don't ever have to hide!
"Stay where you are! Don't move!" he said,
And pressed a button on his head.
At once, there came a blinding flash,
And then the most almighty crash,
And sparks were bursting all around,
And smoke was rising from the ground . . .
When all the smoke had cleared away
The Frenchmen with their knives cried, "*Hey!*
"Where is the toad? Where has he gone?"
You see, I now was sitting on
A wonderfully ENORMOUS SNAIL!
His shell was smooth and brown and pale,
And I was so high off the ground
That I could see for miles around.
The Snail said, "Hello! Greetings! Hail!
"I was a Toad. Now I'm a Snail.
"I had to change the way I looked
"To save myself from being cooked."
"Oh Snail," I said, "I'm not so sure.
"I think they're starting up once more."
The French were shouting, "What a snail!
"Oh, what a monster! What a whale!
"He makes the toad look titchy small!
"There's lovely snail-meat for us all!
"We'll bake the creature in his shell
"And ring aloud the dinner-bell!
"Get garlic, parsley, butter, spices!
"We'll cut him into fifty slices!